Arctic Wolf

The High Arctic

by Laura DeLallo

Consultant: Dean Cluff
Regional Biologist
Environment and Natural Resources
Government of the Northwest Territories

BEARPORT
PUBLISHING

New York, New York

Credits

Cover and Title Page, © Wildlife GmbH/Alamy; TOC, © Denis Pepin/Shutterstock; 4, Courtesy of Dan MacNulty; 5, © NaturePL/SuperStock; 6, © Bruce Corbett/Alamy; 7, Courtesy of Oleg Mikhailov; 8, Courtesy of David Mech/U.S. Geological Survey; 9, © Dave Brosha Photography/Flickr/Getty Images; 10-11, © IndexStock/SuperStock; 12, © John Shaw/NHPA/Photoshot; 13TL, © Accent Alaska/Alamy; 13TR, © Jim Brandenburg/Minden Pictures/Getty Images; 13B, © Thorsten Milse/Mauritius/Photolibrary; 14, © Courtesy of Dean Cluff; 15, Courtesy of Dean Cluff; 16L, © Andy Rouse/NHPA/Photoshot; 16R, © Radius/SuperStock; 17T, © Jim Brandenburg/Minden Pictures/NGS Images; 17B, © Jeff Turner/Nature Picture Library; 18, © Jim Brandenburg/Minden Pictures/NGS Images; 19, © Jim Brandenburg/Minden Pictures/NGS Images; 20, © Jeff Turner/Nature Picture Library; 21T, © Jim Brandenburg/Minden Pictures/Getty Images; 21B, © Jim Brandenburg/Minden Pictures/Getty Images; 22, © Jeff Turner/Nature Picture Library; 23T, © Jim Brandenburg/Minden Pictures/NGS Images; 23B, © Jim Brandenburg/Minden Pictures/NGS Images; 24T, © Jim Brandenburg/Minden Pictures/Getty Images; 24B, © RKS Images/Alamy; 25, © David W. Hamilton/Riser/Getty Images; 26, © Courtesy of Dean Cluff; 27, © NaturePL/SuperStock; 28, © Jim Brandenburg/Minden Pictures/Getty Images; 29T, © Matthias Breiter/Minden Pictures/Getty Images; 29B, © All Canada Photos/SuperStock; 31, © Jeff Grabert/Shutterstock; 32, © Denis Pepin/Shutterstock.

Publisher: Kenn Goin
Senior Editor: Lisa Wiseman
Creative Director: Spencer Brinker
Photo Researcher: Picture Perfect Professionals, LLC

Library of Congress Cataloging-in-Publication Data

DeLallo, Laura.
  Arctic wolf : the high arctic / by Laura DeLallo.
      p. cm. — (Built for the cold: arctic animals)
  Includes bibliographical references and index.
  ISBN-13: 978-1-61772-132-8 (library binding)
  ISBN-10: 1-61772-132-8 (library binding)
  1. Gray wolf—Arctic regions—Juvenile literature. I. Title.
  QL737.C22D46 2011
  599.773—dc22
                                2010037208

For more information, write to Bearport Publishing Company, Inc., 101 Fifth Avenue, Suite 6R, New York, New York 10003. Printed in the United States of America.

10 9 8 7 6 5 4 3 2

Contents

The First Meeting

"Did you hear that?" Dean Cluff asked his coworker Dave Mech. The only thing that Dave could hear was the sound of raindrops pounding on the hood of his poncho. It was around 11:00 at night on July 6, 2009, but it was still light outside. The two **biologists** were sitting atop a rocky hill on Ellesmere Island, Canada, waiting to spot an arctic wolf.

Dean Cluff (left) and Dave Mech (right) on Ellesmere Island

Ellesmere Island is located in the High Arctic—the northernmost part of the **Arctic region**. From mid-April through the end of August, the sun never sets in that part of the Arctic. From late October through mid-February, it never rises.

Suddenly, Dean heard the sound again. Could it be a wolf howling? Then, about 30 minutes later, Dean and Dave saw something white moving toward them. "A wolf!" Dean shouted. Soon they noticed another one not too far behind. Dave and Dean sat very still. The wolves walked right up to them. It was exactly what the scientists were hoping for.

An arctic wolf

No Fear

In most other areas of the world, studying a wolf up close would have been very difficult. Wolves fear humans, who sometimes hunt and kill them for their fur. Other people kill them for **sport**. As a result, wolves don't usually let humans get very close to them.

The arctic wolf gets its name from the area where it lives.

Adult wolves have no natural **predators**. Only humans hunt wolves.

However, the arctic wolves that Dave and Dean study live so far north that they don't see people often enough to be afraid of them. The nearest human community to the wolves is Eureka, a small weather station and military base located a few miles away. Only a handful of people live there year-round.

Arctic Wolves in the Wild

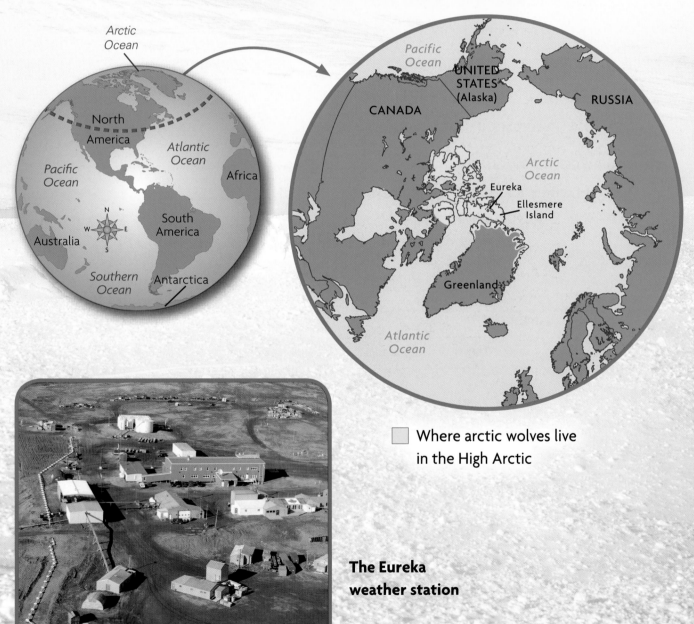

Where arctic wolves live in the High Arctic

The Eureka weather station

Winter Mystery

The wolves that walked up to Dave and Dean in the summer of 2009 were curious but not scared, and neither were the two scientists. Dave had been studying the wolves on Ellesmere Island since 1986. In fact, he was the first scientist to study a wolf that lived so far north. As a result, he knew from his studies that arctic wolves are rarely dangerous to humans. So that's why Dave and Dean just sat calmly on the ground to show that they weren't a **threat**. The wolves sniffed them and moved on.

Dave sits calmly on the ground as two arctic wolf pups approach him.

Dave and Dean wondered how these wolves survived the harsh Arctic winters, which are bitterly cold and dark. Ice and snow cover mountains and valleys. Temperatures can dip as low as −70°F (−57°C). To survive in such an environment, animals need to be able to stay warm enough to move around and hunt for food.

The snow-covered Arctic

Few people live in the Arctic year-round because it is too cold. Dave and many other scientists usually visit the Arctic in the summer, when temperatures rise to about 65°F (18°C).

Adapting to the Cold

Arctic wolves are physically well **adapted** to their freezing world. Two layers of thick fur cover their bodies. A woolly undercoat keeps the animals warm while the long hairs of the outercoat protect them from rain and snow.

The wolves' bodies have adapted to the cold in other ways, too. Their **muzzles**, legs, and ears are shorter than the same body parts found on wolves living in warmer areas. As a result, these body parts are close to an arctic wolf's chest and stomach, which are the center of heat in its body. This helps a wolf stay warm.

Arctic wolves even have fur between the pads on the bottoms of their paws. It keeps their paws warm as they walk over frozen ground.

Throughout the winter, even during heavy snowstorms, the wolf's thick coat keeps it warm.

Frozen Food

Arctic wolves need more than thick coats to survive the winter. They also need to find food so they won't **starve** to death. Fortunately, wolves have white coats that help them blend in with their snowy surroundings while hunting. This **camouflage** allows them to get close to **prey** without being seen.

An arctic wolf blends into the white snow, making it easier for it to sneak up on prey.

Wolves on Ellesmere Island mostly hunt plant-eating animals, such as arctic hares, caribou, and musk oxen. During the winter, when plants are buried under snow and ice, the plant-eaters have a hard time finding food. Without enough to eat, many of them die of starvation or become too weak to run away or defend themselves from predators. They are then easy prey for the wolves. However, if too many of these animals die from lack of food, the wolves themselves face starvation.

Like arctic wolves, musk oxen (left) and caribou (right) have two layers of fur to help keep them warm.

The arctic hares that live on Ellesmere Island don't turn brown like hares in warmer areas. Their fur stays white all year long. Scientists think the reason for this is that the short summer season isn't enough time for their fur to change to brown and then back to white before the land is covered with snow again.

Help from Brutus

In July 2009, Dave and Dean were on a mission to find out what it takes for wolves to find **scarce** prey during the long Arctic winters. To do this, they put a special collar on Brutus, one of the wolves they had recently seen near Eureka. The collar held a tiny computer that recorded Brutus's location every 12 hours and sent the information to a **satellite**. Dave and Dean then downloaded the locations from the satellite to their home computers all winter long. From the comfort of their homes, they were able to keep track of Brutus's movements.

Before Dave, shown here, put the special collar around Brutus's neck, Dean gave the wolf a drug to make him go to sleep.

From previous studies, Dave and Dean knew that wolves don't have a **permanent** home once their pups are old enough to travel. They continually **roam** their **territory**, looking for food. However, the scientists discovered something surprising as they studied Brutus's movements. He went far beyond his usual territory in search of prey, even crossing frozen seawater to hunt on other islands.

Brutus wearing the collar

An arctic wolf's territory during the winter is usually about 250 to 500 square miles (647 to 1,295 sq km). Between July 9 and November 30, 2010, Brutus covered an area that was more than 949 square miles (2,458 sq km).

Surviving the Winter

Like all arctic wolves, Brutus was well adapted for traveling long distances in harsh winter conditions. His large, strong feet allowed him to run for long periods of time without tiring. His flexible toes helped him climb rocky hills covered in snow. His strong legs let him run quickly through snow.

Arctic wolves can travel up to 5 miles per hour (8 kph) for long periods of time. When chasing prey, they can run up to 38 miles per hour (61 kph) for short periods of time.

An arctic wolf is able to easily climb rocky hills.

Wolves like Brutus also have something else that helps them survive in their **environment**—other wolves. During the winter they live in large **packs** of up to 30 animals. Living this way allows the wolves to find more food. On hunts, the pack sometimes breaks into smaller groups. Splitting up into smaller groups lets the wolves cover more areas in search of prey. It also gives them the chance to watch their prey from different angles. Once a group finds food, they share it with the rest of the pack.

These wolves use their noses to sniff for prey.

Arctic wolves sharing a meal

Wolves use their powerful senses to find food. They can smell prey from more than one mile (1.6 km) away and they can hear sounds from as far away as ten miles (16 km).

We Are Family

Members of a wolf pack are usually members of the same family. A pack that Dave studied in 1986, long before he met Brutus, included a mother and a father. Dave suspected that the five other wolves in the pack were the parents' older **offspring**.

An arctic wolf pack

In the spring of 1986, Dave followed the pack as they found a huge rock cave to use as a **den**. They needed it because the mother was about to give birth to six little pups. Baby wolves are born deaf and blind and their fur is thin. It takes at least 12 weeks for them to grow big enough to travel with the pack. So a den provides a warm safe place for the pups until they are old enough to travel with their family.

Three-week-old pups sleeping in a den

Pups don't open their eyes until they are two weeks old. They don't see well until weeks later. Pups cannot hear until they are about three weeks old.

Feeding the Family

During his time with the family, Dave watched the wolves raise their pups. For the first three weeks, the mother wolf fed her pups by letting them drink milk from her body. Then, when they were old enough to eat solid food, the pack began to bring meat to them.

At about seven weeks old, pups begin taking short walks with adults.

Dave was curious about how the pack hunted for food. So one day he followed the adult wolves as they left the den. After some time had passed, they found a **herd** of musk oxen. The wolves immediately rushed toward the herd, causing the oxen to run. Once the mother wolf grabbed a **calf**, some of the other wolves jumped on the animal to push it down to the ground. By the end of the day, the pack had caught two more calves.

Arctic wolves chasing a herd of musk oxen

An arctic wolf attacking a musk ox

An adult musk ox weighs between 400 and 600 pounds (181 and 272 kg). Calves make easier prey for wolves because they are smaller and slower than adult musk oxen.

Eat, Sleep, Play

All together the three calves that the wolves caught on their hunt weighed more than 300 pounds (136 kg). The pack ate some of the meat from their kill right away. They buried the rest of it for later use in holes that they dug in the ground called **caches**. Then everyone rested before returning to the den.

When the pups saw the adults coming back, they ran up to them with their tails wagging. To feed the pups, the adults threw up some of the food they had just eaten. The pups gulped it down.

Adult arctic wolves need up to five pounds (2.3 kg) of meat a day to survive. Young wolves need to eat even more than that to be able to grow quickly before winter comes.

After eating, they went back to playing and sleeping, which is how growing pups spend most of their time. Sleeping helps their bodies grow stronger. Play fighting with one another helps them learn to **compete** for food in the wild. About five months after they're born, the pups begin to go on real hunts with the pack.

Pups love to play fight with one another.

Pups gain about 3 pounds (1.4 kg) per week. They can weigh more than 50 pounds (23 kg) before they are four months old.

Playing tires the pups out.

Growing Up

Besides sleeping, eating, and playing, pups also practice howling. Wolves generally howl to let members of their pack know where they are. They also howl to let others from different packs know they're not welcome in their territory. Sometimes, however, wolves howl just for fun.

A pup howling

A person can hear a wolf howl from more than five miles (8 km) away.

Pups become full-size adults when they're around two years old. By then, they know how to hunt, howl, and survive in the cold Arctic. Young wolves stay with their parents for one to three years. Then some leave the pack to find a **mate** and create their own pack.

Wolves start to have pups of their own when they are about three years old.

Brutus and Beyond

Through their research of the wolves on Ellesmere Island, both Dave and Dean have learned a lot about these amazing Arctic animals. Unfortunately, their study of Brutus ended in April 2010, when the information from his collar showed that something was wrong. His location hadn't changed for several days. Dave and Dean realized that ten-year-old Brutus had most likely died. He had lived a long life for an arctic wolf. Most wolves in the wild don't live to see age ten.

Scientists can learn a wolf's age by studying its teeth. Older wolves' teeth show more wear than those of younger wolves.

Dave studying the wear on Brutus's teeth

Brutus and other Ellesmere Island wolves have taught researchers a lot about their lives. Today Dave and Dean continue to study arctic wolves, some that are even Brutus's relatives. They also inform other researchers about wolves. They hope to put a collar on another wolf on Ellesmere Island one day. There is still a lot to learn about this cool Arctic predator.

Arctic Wolf Facts

With two layers of fur and powerful senses for hunting, the arctic wolf is perfectly adapted for life in the Arctic. Here are some other facts about these amazing animals.

Weight	male adults weigh from 75 to 125 pounds (34 to 57 kg); female adults weigh only slightly less
Length	3 to 5 feet (.9 to 1.5 m), including the tail
Height	26 to 32 inches (66 to 81 cm) at the shoulder
Food	mainly musk oxen, caribou, and arctic hares, but they will also eat mouse-like animals called lemmings, birds, and seals when they get the chance
Life Span	about 7 to 10 years in the wild; up to 17 years in zoos
Habitat	Arctic region
Population	Scientists don't know the exact number, but they think there are about 200 wolves living in the High Arctic.

More Arctic Animals

The Arctic region is one of the harshest **habitats** on Earth. Only animals that are adapted to extreme cold, such as the arctic wolf, can survive there. Here are two other Arctic survivors.

Musk Ox

- There are about 125,000 musk oxen living in the Arctic.
- They eat grasses, mosses, and plant roots. In winter, musk oxen use their hooves to dig out frozen plants from beneath ice and snow.
- Humans, wolves, and bears are the musk oxen's main predators.

- When a predator tries to attack musk oxen, the animals form a circle. The adult oxen put their calves in the middle of the circle and stand with their heads and sharp horns facing out.

Arctic Hare

- Arctic hares are the largest hares in the world. They are about two feet (61 cm) long and weigh about 12 pounds (5.4 kg).
- They eat mostly twigs, grasses, and flowers.
- They sit on their legs and flatten their ears against their heads to stay warm.

- They can run up to 40 miles per hour (64 kph) to escape from predators such as the arctic wolf and the arctic fox.

Glossary

adapted (uh-DAP-tid) changed over time to survive in an environment

Arctic region (ARK-tik REE-juhn) the northernmost area on Earth; it includes the Arctic Ocean, the North Pole, and northern parts of Europe, Asia, and North America, and is one of the coldest areas in the world

biologists (bye-OL-uh-jists) scientists who study plants or animals

caches (KASH-iz) hiding places for supplies of food that are stored for later use

calf (KAF) the young of some large animals, such as cows and musk oxen

camouflage (KAM-uh-flahzh) a covering or coloring that makes people or animals blend into their surroundings

compete (kuhm-PEET) to try hard to get something that others are also trying to get

den (DEN) an animal's home; a hidden place where an animal sleeps and has its babies

environment (en-VYE-ruhn-muhnt) the area where an animal or plant lives, and all the things, such as weather, that affect the place

habitats (HAB-uh-tats) places in the wild where animals or plants normally live

herd (HURD) a large group of animals that live together

mate (MATE) one of a pair of animals that have young together

muzzles (MUHZ-ulz) the noses, mouths, and jaws of some animals, such as wolves

offspring (OF-spring) the young of a person or animal

packs (PAKS) groups of one kind of animal

permanent (PUR-muh-nuhnt) created to last forever

predators (PRED-uh-turz) animals that hunt and kill other animals for food

prey (PRAY) animals that are hunted or caught for food

roam (ROHM) to wander around

satellite (SAT-uh-lite) a spacecraft that is placed in orbit and is able to send information back to Earth

scarce (SKAIRSS) hard to find because there's so little of it

sport (SPORT) a particular activity that is done for fun

starve (STARV) to die from lack of food

territory (TER-uh-tor-ee) an area of land lived on and defended by an animal or a group of animals

threat (THRET) something that might cause harm

Bibliography

Fuller, Todd K. *Wolves of the World.* Stillwater, MN: Voyageur Press (2004).

Mech, L. David. *The Arctic Wolf: Living with the Pack.* Stillwater, MN: Voyageur Press (1988).

Mech, L. David. *The Way of the Wolf.* Stillwater, MN: Voyageur Press (1991).

internationalwolfcenter.blogspot.com

www.wolf.org

Read More

Brandenburg, Jim and Judy. *Face to Face with Wolves.* Washington, D.C.: National Geographic Children's Books (2010).

Goldish, Meish. *Gray Wolves (America's Animal Comebacks).* New York: Bearport (2008).

Simon, Seymour. *Wolves.* New York: HarperCollins Publishers (2009).

Sisk, Maeve T. *Arctic Wolves.* New York: Gareth Stevens Publishing (2010).

Learn More Online

To learn more about arctic wolves, visit
www.bearportpublishing.com/BuiltforCold

Index

About the Author

Laura DeLallo has written several children's books and has had international success as a singer and songwriter. She lives with her family in Stamford, Connecticut.